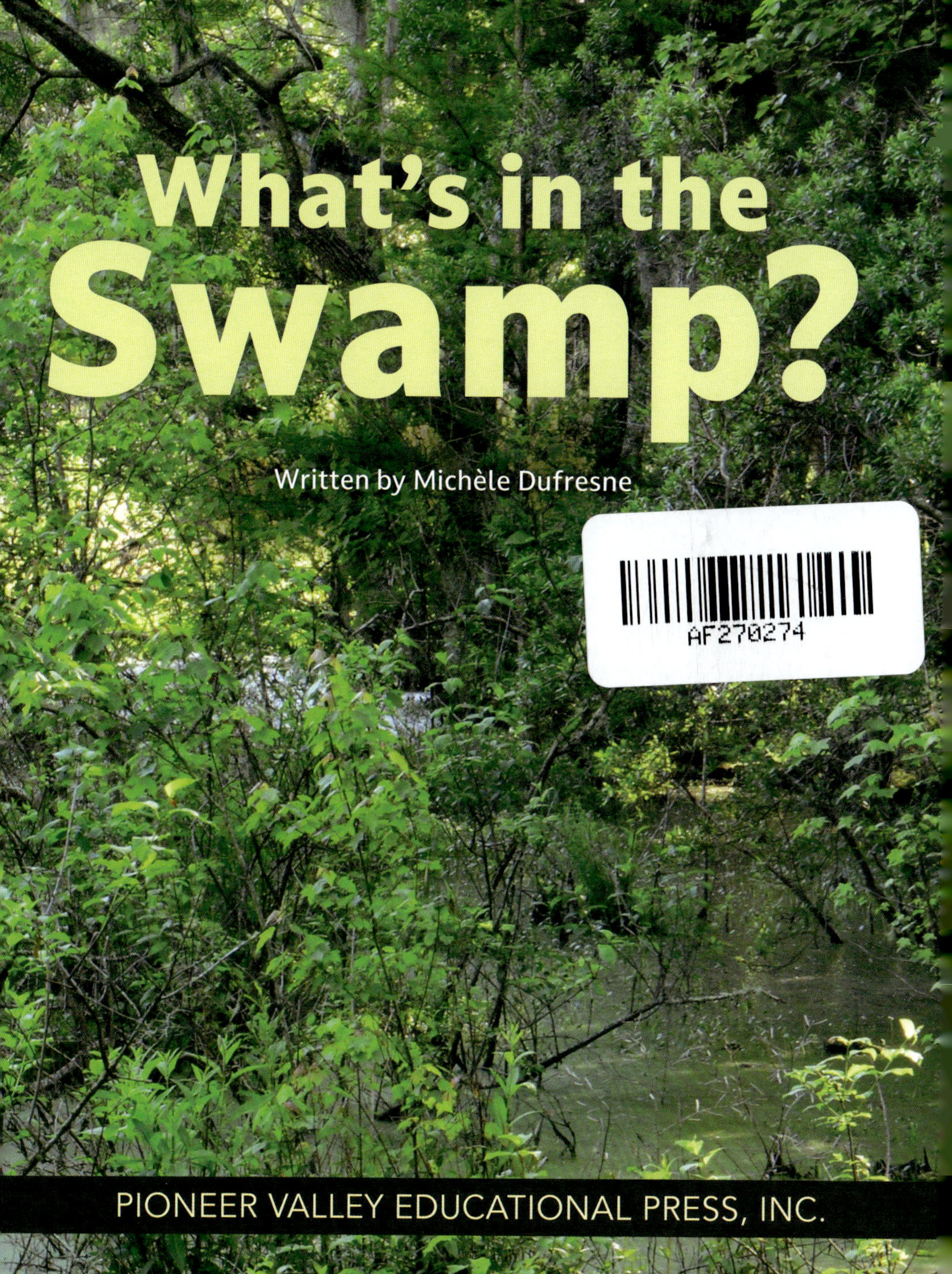

What's in the
Swamp?
Written by Michèle Dufresne
PIONEER VALLEY EDUCATIONAL PRESS, INC.

This is a swamp.

The swamp is thick
with bushes and grass.

A swamp is a forested wetland. Swamps can be found all over the world.

Let's chop down
some bushes.
Now we have a thin path.
What can we see
in the swamp?

Swamps are very wet. This is why
trails that run through swamps
are often made with planks.

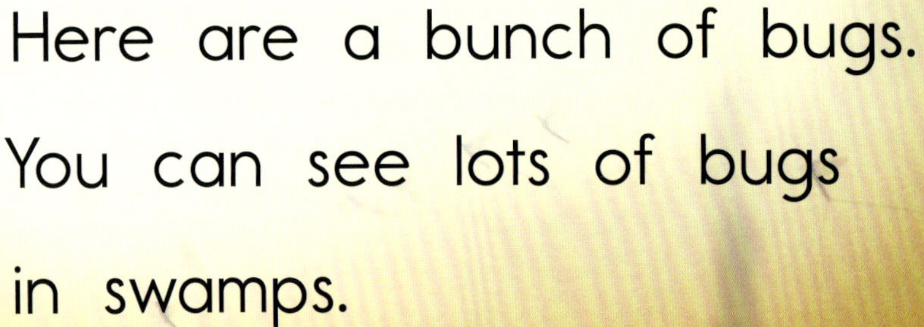

Here are a bunch of bugs. You can see lots of bugs in swamps.

Wet swamps make a great home for insects. Many mosquitoes live in swamps. They like to lay their eggs in standing water.

Can you see the fish?

Look at it swim

in the swamp.

It has **whiskers**

on its chin.

Swamps are home to many fish. One kind of fish that lives in swamps is the catfish. Catfish use their whiskers to find food in the dark, murky water.

Can you spot

the **alligator**?

It can see the fish.

Snip, snap!

The alligator shuts its **jaw**

with a big snap!

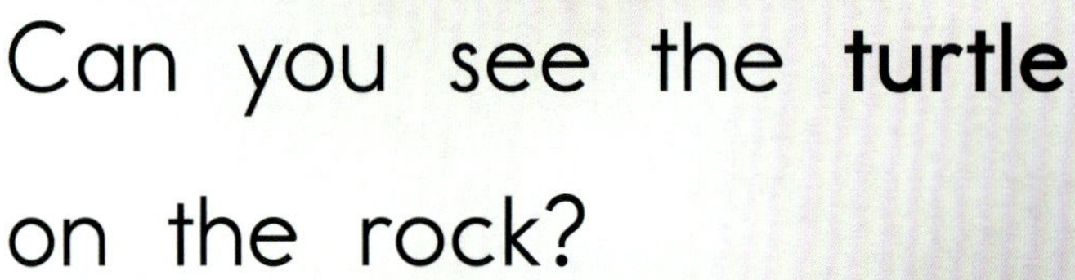

Can you see the **turtle** on the rock? Check out the red on the turtle's shell.

Many kinds of turtles live in swamps. This is a painted turtle. Painted turtles have brightly colored shells.

glossary